Soul ON THE RUN

WHAT READERS SAY

"Many years ago I identified the possibility of living a new reality, but often missed the mark of getting there. Through self-discovery and acceptance, it was attainable. It is attainable by all. Robin Korth's lasted book does just that for her readers; allowing the reader to rediscover the real self, unmasking the false reality that was once before them. Through her un-filtered approach to her personal understanding, she shares an easier understanding for us all. As the pages turn, we are challenged to try something new. While not telling us what to do, she takes our hands through a personal journey we call our own."

--Joseph Lieungh
Life Coach, Author, Speaker

"She instantly connects with the reader, forcing a hard look at what is important in life."

--Fred Kelleher
Hobe Sound, FL

"[Robin] has taught me through laughter and sometimes tears of recognition, my own unseen truths."

--Kathleen Parvin
Endicott, NY

Soul ON THE RUN

ROBIN KORTH

BALBOA
PRESS

A DIVISION OF HAY HOUSE

Balboa Press books may be ordered through booksellers or by contacting:

Balboa Press
A Division of Hay House
1663 Liberty Drive
Bloomington, IN 47403
www.balboapress.com
1 (877) 407-4847

Because of the dynamic nature of the Internet, any web addresses or
links contained in this book may have changed since publication and
may no longer be valid. The views expressed in this work are solely those
of the author and do not necessarily reflect the views of the publisher,
and the publisher hereby disclaims any responsibility for them.

The author of this book does not dispense medical advice or prescribe the use
of any technique as a form of treatment for physical, emotional, or medical
problems without the advice of a physician, either directly or indirectly. The
intent of the author is only to offer information of a general nature to help you
in your quest for emotional and spiritual well-being. In the event you use any
of the information in this book for yourself, which is your constitutional right,
the author and the publisher assume no responsibility for your actions.

Any people depicted in stock imagery provided by Thinkstock are models,
and such images are being used for illustrative purposes only.
Certain stock imagery © Thinkstock.

Printed in the United States of America.

ISBN: 978-1-4525-9098-1 (sc)
ISBN: 978-1-4525-9100-1 (e)

Library of Congress Control Number: 2014901256

Balboa Press rev. date: 2/12/2014

This book is dedicated to the human race with laughter, joy, honesty and courage. Let us truly realize and know that we are remarkable, amazing and beautiful. We are also so very, very powerful.

FOREWORD

By Jean Houston

Robin Korth, a woman at once both primal and profound, here launches the crazy wisdom of her trenchant mind. Her readers will never be the same. "Why didn't I ever say that, think that, do that?" cries the reader. Or even sadder yet, "Why didn't I live deep enough, fierce enough, and with radical self-knowledge so as to see more sharply and then live more powerfully?"

This is not an innocent book. It brooks no whiney nay-saying. You are brought up short by the honesty to yourself that it demands. The potent and passionate anecdotes and challenges that form its necklace of life seeds are discoveries of the hidden self, uncomfortable as that may be.

But make no mistake, in entering into this work, the mind is plowed so as to be more fertile. The soul is fished to be more available. And finally, life with all its warts and wonders is revealed, and you find that you are more than you pretend to be. You are the God in hiding, the Cosmos in a fractal of itself, exploring its own nature in a limited time and space vehicle, the Universe in miniature.

Robin's words echo Auntie Mame, who proclaimed, "Life is a banquet and most poor suckers are starving to death!" I knew Auntie Mame, the real one, immortalized by her nephew Patrick Dennis in his book about her magnificent, if eccentric, lifestyle. Her real name was Marion Tanner. When I was about 20, I met her, and she engaged me in helping her pick up Bowery bums, alcoholic down-and-outers, and bring them to her Greenwich Village home for care and rehabilitation. She was even greater than her portrayal in book and movie, a true original who lived life fully and cared so gorgeously for those who had forgotten the banquet. She brought them back to the feast.

Robin looks a little like her, tall and willowy, her face a landscape of rich expression, her mind like Marion's, ever curious, questing, facing hard issues of self and society, never giving up and always, always, inviting us to the feast.

INTRODUCTION

I am a renegade and an outlaw. Born to a large family with quick pride and deep hearts, I always wanted to color outside the lines and dance to a different tune. From my first memories, this soul of mine has called to the earth and whispered to the clouds. My mind has been a quicksilver place of questions, connections, ideas, insights and fantasies. I grabbed life. I lusted it and then I mis-lived it. And the hand that held the blade of my destruction was always my own.

I am a survivor of my own poorly-managed, sad, outrageous and courageous attempt to do life alone—to do life as an independent operator. For you see, this is what I was taught. To do life you must fight, you must win, and you must be the best. You need to follow the rules and follow the leader. Do not question your world too much. Get it done, get the guy, get the job, the house, the car, the family, the goodies and all will be well.

But it wasn't. Not for me. I wanted more. My heart called and my soul cried. I could not find peace or meaning or a place within a regular sort of life. As I look back now, I can see I was never meant to fit that mold. I did not get it or it simply didn't get me. I had an empty spot. There was a place that needed filling—a place that left me questing and questioning.

Through so much of my life, there was no Robin at the center of me. I was a soul on the run. A bird meant to fly that had no idea that wings are not just given, they are created and gifted to ourselves only after much work, deep passion, pure-hot desire and a willingness to take the strafing that life gives with gratitude and acceptance. Wings come to those who take the journey to heal the wounds, to mend the heart and to reach beyond a limited version of living.

So it was in 2006 that I finally began my journey towards flight. I turned away from life as I was supposed to love it. I reached and stretched, I read and questioned, I angered and I eagered. I howled for a God and reached for a purpose. I hungered for more than what was on the table of my life, my history, my self.

This was the cry of my brokenness—a brokenness that did not just happen. It was there all the time, grinding and working, creaking and shaking. My history is rife with the strewn nuts and bolts, the bits and pieces of me: the little girl, the proud dancer, the mighty intellect, the grief-ridden child, the self-sure arrogant and the anger-spitting shrew.

In fear and searching for comfort, I turned to anorexia and bulimia at age fourteen. For forty years I binged and I puked. I gourmet cooked and I stuffed. I threw up and filled my proud-flat stomach with food again. Time is easily filled with constant attention to a belly never allowed satisfaction by a heart that doesn't know it is lost. At five-foot-nine, I weighed 104 pounds the year I turned thirty-three. My teeth decayed and dissolved. I was a walking testimony to a broken soul. But all I saw in the mirror was a size-four set of hips.

In my twenties, I grew a business and broke gender barriers. I played with government undercover operatives and criminals in the hide-and-seek games that were Miami during the "Cocaine Cowboy" days of the late 1970s and early 1980s. I fell in love with the "wrong" guy and knew it from the start. But my heart was tagged by a passionate need for this man that would haunt me and hold me for more than twenty-nine years.

With adventures thrilling, sorrowful and quietly lonely, I rode the train of my life into my thirties thinking I had a clue of what I was doing. In 1984, I gave birth to our first daughter. A year later, I buried our second. I was taught to keep marching no matter what. So march I did—reaching for a new version of me as I went—thinking each time I had found a Robin that would fit. As I rolled close to forty, our son was born and I decided it was time to "settle in" for the duration of my days.

This meant that I set out to get the life that Ozzie and Harriet had modeled—the one my parents and siblings seem to find whole and worthy. So the days of do-over living began. I tried. Dear God, I did try. But it was all somehow a horrible game of let's pretend. Let's pretend I am happy. Let's pretend this makes sense. I was a character actor in the figment of an imagined "good life" that was hollow at the core and had seams that ripped when tugged. I was a lost girl wandering the stage of what was supposed to be my life.

Desperate for a sense of self, I went back to school at age thirty-nine in 1994. I had always shone and succeeded in academia since the letter "A" first came from my child-fisted hand. So I returned to a place that made sense—a place where there was order and meaning, classes to attend and research to do. But this didn't fill the hole in my soul any more than the food-stuffing did. It was time for alcohol to join the mix. It did a goodly job of giving me numbed days and tear-sodden, passed-out nights for a decade or more. Until it didn't work anymore and I wanted it done.

But the booze wasn't done with me. The bulimia wasn't done with me. My delusion that I had any idea that I really knew how to live wasn't done with me. My close-minded arrogance and spirit-lostness wasn't done with me. I was totally unable to let go of the idea that I could "fix" myself. The messages of my childhood, my "can-do" culture and my own pride had me strapped tight in a horror ride of "tomorrow will be better" self-delusion.

These self-hewn death straps finally began to let go of me on a day in 2006 when I let go. I was standing in front of my bathroom mirror on a Miami winter's day. I looked fully into my own eyes, and for the first time in my entire life, I actually clearly saw *me*. I was angry, sad, lost, disappointed, sniveling and resentful. I was also fifty-one years old with my youth gone and possibly another thirty years more to go. The thought of living those years feeling as I did took my breath with a gut punch of terror. And from the clarity of this one defining moment, came choice and action.

I turned from my reflection and began the journey into learning how to truly live. I had to find this lady called Robin who had been walking around in this body of mine for half a century. I had to go on a search and destroy mission and then a creation mission. I had to get honest and tear the blinders off. I had to call myself on my own lies and tell myself the truth. I had to get real and start making good decisions and get my butt off the sidewalk of my own life. I had to stop feeling sorry for myself and start taking care of myself. I asked for help and I took it. I shut my mouth and opened my heart. I opened my mind and worked to turn on my soul. As I moved forward day after day—change by small change—life began to take on meaning and power. There was a sense of joy coming through and a sense of wonder walking with me. My soul was no longer on the run. I had come home to me. I had at last shown up in my own life.

There were many bumps and bruises along the way. There were more than a few easy-out sneaky side paths and attempted short-cuts that did not work. But today my feet, my heart, my mind and my spirit are doing a touring ride through this adventure of living. I ache and I breathe life. I read and I question. I see and I love. The hours of my days are filled with eager reaching and gentle holding. They are filled with my spirit full-on laughing into this gift of being alive.

And it is from this journey of now that the thoughts and words, insights and ideas, the clarity and joy of this book were born. I have spent the last seven years since that day in front of the mirror on a journey towards truth. The seeking and the finding of what drives me—what drives us—as human beings. I have become a student of life and a craving soul of the power that creates us. It is a "God" thing that calls me. But not a God of any book or missal, not a God of a philosopher or a preacher, not a God of an oath or a curse. It is a God of me meeting the universe soul-wide and spirit broad.

Some may say I blaspheme or who do I think I am. Who is this woman who dares to speak with such a sure voice and such a clear heart? I am. I am a woman who walked into living torn open by the despair of my own choices and the damage of years of not knowing how to live. This pain and this sorrow flayed me and left me willing to start looking at what is really going on in life—to look behind the scenes of every day. There is ever so much more than we realize. But it takes courage and need. It takes passion and desire. It takes a questing heart—and a spirit that is willing to be bruised and broken—as we let go of our illusions and stand full-tall in our own lives.

We need to be honest—terribly, brutally honest—with ourselves. We need to stop playing "let's pretend it is all okay," and get really busy being real and raw, gutsy and self-good. We need to claim our birthright. That birthright is one of joy, a self-created life, a blowing spirit and a richness and fullness that is endless. We are meant to be happy and whole, joy-calling and bright, rich and deep, powerful and profound. We are.

I am you and the person beside you. I am beautiful and remarkable and amazing. I am powerful, self-creating and soul-starred. So are you. So are we all. Each of us creates our lives. Each of us stands at the edge of the world with the power of creation within us. We are the life. We are God's gift. We are His echo and His song. We are His joy and His laughter.

We are!

INSTRUCTIONS FOR USE

This book is me on the half-page. This is a collection of thoughts, insights and questions about life and love, growth, laughter and change that accompanied me as I launched myself into living an awake and aware life.

There is no one way—no one-size-fits-all instruction manual—to turn our spirits on as we come fully awake to ourselves in this miracle of life. We each must find our own way. We each must question and seek. We must trust our own thirst for meaning as we follow where that takes us.

Perhaps my thoughts will echo with you, perhaps they will push you and poke you. Perhaps you will see yourself in me. Perhaps your own questions will rise, your heart will tick, "yes!" If this happens, then I have done my job well. For that is what it is all about—the questions, the search, the journey, the adventure.

May your journey be uncomfortable, inquisitive, honest and brave. For therein, you will begin to find yourself, your life, your freedom and your joy.

The joy isn't *in* the journey. It *is* the journey.

ON THIS DAY, I wish you a true knowing that you are amazing and beautiful. I wish you peace and compassion. I wish you self-honesty and the courage to stand tall and claim the soul that sparks within you. I wish you understanding and delight. I wish you challenges that push your heart to grow and sing. But most of all, I wish you to know that you are not alone, that my laughter and my joy walk with you.

If I knew then what I know now, I would not have had a clue what to do with the information.

People seldom improve when they have no role model but themselves.

In our fear or pride, we refuse to tell another that we are scared, suffering and alone. And in refusing to share our pain, so do we remain—scared, suffering and alone.

I lived scared for years, alone and sure I was a failure in my own life. I was quiet in my desperate unhappiness. I tried to find meaning in being "good" and in being there for others. But this didn't work.

Why? I had no clue who I really was. So being there for others was just another game upon the game of me pretending. I did not see this, so I tried and tried, and I failed and I failed.

It is only now that I actually have come to accept and like the *all* of me—warts, talents, personal faults and personal gifts—that I know who I am. So I can throw all I've got at life, including being there for others. And I can do it with a wide open grin, an open heart and a laughing soul.

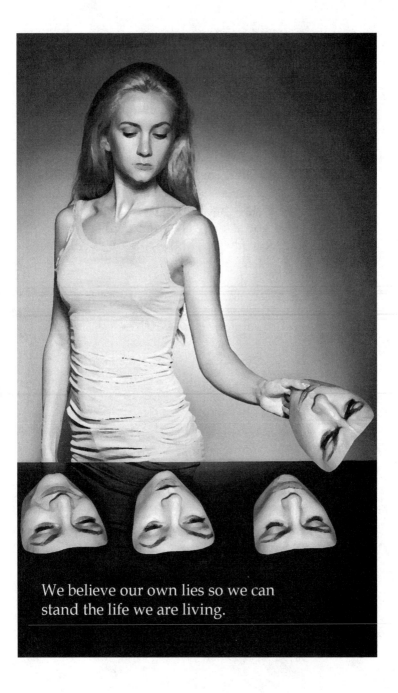

We believe our own lies so we can
stand the life we are living.

Let us not bow our heads. Let us not think we don't matter. Let us not say, "I can't." We are capable of so very, very much in our lives. And this "much" is often found in what we might view as the little things.

We can ease another's pain by listening. We can call our voice to the truth even though we may be speaking alone. We can reach our heart out to another in the power of a shared smile.

We are amazing and so very beautiful and we so rarely claim the true wonder of all that we are. We are this remarkably frail and extraordinarily strong creature—a human being.

For me, spiritual living is not incense and candles. It is an in-the-trenches, core-deep connection to those around me. It is a quiet heart and a soul that listens. It is an openness to the pace and pulse of the world. It is also a willingness to get dirty and raw, to cry and to share in the hurts and the joys of those around me.

As I age time has become an interesting companion—a smaller and nearer friend. I now hold its hand in each moment because the years are roaring by like a freight train.

My God created me gut-level, earthy and very real. So for me, any true connection to Him must be gut-level, earthy and very real.

Confidence and failure are deeply intertwined. It is the knowing—spiritually, mentally and physically—that we have been somewhere before, taken the hit, and survived, that gives us the calm willingness to walk into the challenges of life yet again.

Soul-caught. It is the spent sigh of a mother closing a sleeping child's bedroom door. It is the aching intimacy passed in a quiet glance between two lovers. It is the smile of delight on a face upturned to the sun. It is the wide-grinned welcome of a man crouched with arms wide ready to catch the body of his barreling dog. It is the whoosh-plash of the wind as it kisses the trees. My soul is caught. It is totally and completely caught by this gift. This life.

The day I learned to cry with my head up was the day I knew it was all going to be okay. I understood that my tears were the same as yours; the same as everyone's who has ever cried.

Why *not* me?

Why do we bemoan death and think it the worst tragedy? Without it, life makes no sense at all.

I can be selfish, arrogant, a know-it-all, impatient, judgmental, a blabber mouth and insensitive. Isn't this just wonderful? Look at all the stuff I have that I can work on.

<u>A CHALLENGE:</u> Take a good look at yourself today. Make an inventory of some of the crappy stuff you don't like about yourself. Are these things so *very* terrible? Are they not simply human qualities gone a bit awry? Are they worth the pain they cause you? How do they make you feel about yourself? How would you feel if you changed them?

I don't know about you, but trying to love everyone and spread joyful compassion and loving kindness wherever I went wore the heck out of me.

This was because I hadn't a real clue what I was talking about. It was all words and huge phony-baloney effort. But now that I have come to truly love myself, my love for others is simply part of the whole deal and it just flows.

My God isn't good at beating His head against my denial, laziness, self-entitlement or self-pity. He is really, really good at meeting me halfway, grabbing my hand and saying, "Let's go!"

Heaven is where your feet are.

If I spend all my time worried about you, then I don't have to pay attention to me at all. Very cool diversion tactic. Yes?

For years and years I held on to my anger, my self-pity, my sadness and my despair. I was terrified to let them go, you see. For these bitter parts of me defined me, even as they were slowly killing me.

If I let them go, then who would I be? I was so very used to hanging on to life by my fingernails, looking for meaning with a grit-toothed smile upon my face.

At last that smile tore into a full out cry of anguish as I admitted to myself that I had no clue how to live. I had no clue how to be happy. I had no clue how to love or like myself.

And so, my journey started.

ON THIS DAY, I wish you the courage and honesty to see yourself as you are meant to be. I wish you the willingness to tear off the blinders as you stretch your mind and heart to this adventure. I wish you laughter and energy as you go for the ride of your life. I wish you tears and smiles, challenges and growth, love and ache. For to live life open and brave, free and clear, is the gift that only you can give to yourself.

If I am the same person this evening as I was this morning, I haven't been paying attention.

For me, the most amazing gift of my humanity are my faults and failings. For these create the "working ground" for change. I can choose which ones no longer serve me and let them go. And in doing so the beauty and the power of me doing life—*consciously* choosing who I wish to be—rocks my world, tickles my grin and causes my soul to rise.

One step at a time, one thought at a time, I started being fully honest with myself about myself. And I started choosing how I wanted to live and how I wanted to show up in my own life. I still do this each day, and guess what? My life is amazing now, because it is mine.

My life gets wacky and not pretty when I am in fear. This fear most often does not arise from an outside condition, place or experience. It comes quite simply and powerfully because I am confused or floundering and I have lost track of who I am—what I stand for, my self-core.

I now know this fear to actually be a blessing, for it tells me that it is time for me to get to work and carefully and thoughtfully look for the truth of myself once again.

Life has absolutely no meaning but that which we give to it in our own minds. We create it magnificently or destroy it mightily simply in the way we think about it.

<u>A CHALLENGE:</u> Pay attention to yourself today. Make note of your own behavior and consciously choose to do something differently just for today. Own this choice and feel the power of *you* actually creating who you want to be. Pay attention to how this feels deep down. You like yourself more, don't you?

Hell is being miserable and trying to convince myself and others that I am okay with it.

No one has ever taught me anything, though many have shown me. I must grab on to what I wish to learn—who and what I wish to become—and run with it. I must eat it, breathe it and live it. Then it becomes simply and beautifully who I am.

The line between laughter and tears is an attitude.

It's hard to lie to ourselves
in the shower.

Two of the most courageous and empowering phrases in the world: "I don't know how" and "please show me."

Life is in the doing *and* the dreaming.

Most of my life was a battle—to win, to be better, bigger, stronger, smarter, cooler, simply "more" than you. Why? Because if I was truly honest with myself, I always felt I was "less" than you.

My life was an exhausting battlefield of shoring up my ego by beating others. And even when I had won, I had to be ever-alert for the next onslaught of the save-my-self-esteem war.

It was not until I truly came to accept that I am okay just as I am—warts and wonders all—that I could put the weapons down and begin to simply breathe my own life. What a relief!

ON THIS DAY, let's misbehave. Let's toss our smiles and souls to one another and say, "Yeah!" Let's hold onto our hearts as we jump full-on into the wonder that is us walking this planet. Let's look into one another's eyes and say, "Hello, welcome to my life!" and really, really mean it.

Let's share our joy and our pain. Let's call ourselves to the universe and raise our voices. Let's stand shoulder to shoulder and do this day together, giving it everything we've got.

Isn't it interesting when someone points out your faults and you agree with them, how they get really, really quiet?

Now that I truly understand that my life is a holy experience, I can no longer spit on it, deny it or walk away from it.

When I lived my life by following an outside set of prescribed rules, my life was a "me marching to your drum" deal. It was hollow and shallow. For I was marching to your beat, don't you see?

When I at last understood that this is *my* life, *my* adventure, *my* time on this earth, then I had to create the rules. I had to decide what was valid and true and worth doing.

This also demanded that I come fully awake and shoulder the responsibility—and the joy—of doing my life well for *me*. And in doing this, I can now throw everything I have at being of assistance to you.

So often we do not open the door to the next adventure in our lives because we fear the change that walking through the door will demand of us. So we stay as we are.

A CHALLENGE: What door have you chosen to not open in your life? What are you being called to do that you keep turning from, closing the door on? Open that door in your imagination and take a real heart-look. How does it feel and taste and smell? Perhaps today is the day to make the decision to walk through the door.

Life is not *supposed* to hurt. It really isn't.

My mother's unwitting sins were visited upon me. I was handed her view of life and the rules she strode by. I can continue her march or choose which parts of her legacy I wish to hold and which parts I wish to discard.

In knowing that each person I shall meet this day is in my life for a reason, as I am in theirs, my entire day becomes a series of holy encounters.

Dearest friend: it is not my job to make you happy, to fix you or to complete you. I will stand beside you, though, with my heart full of love and understanding as you work to find your own way.

So often we don't really know our own truth. It gets shaded and kind of dusty on the shelves of our minds. But when we are asked to share ourselves with others, it becomes so much clearer. For in pulling the words from our hearts and owning the facts of our souls, the reality of us shows up.

It is often what we don't say, and what we don't do, that shouts our character most clearly to the world.

As I grow older, I know that truly nothing in life is guaranteed. So each moment is to be treasured and each person cherished. For what I thoughtlessly believed was forever, is often gone in the blink of an eye.

Ask, and I will help you any way I can. Demand, and I must walk away. If I comply with your selfish needs, I actually am party to the quiet destruction of your soul. And this I cannot be.

Our journey towards self calls us to rise and claim the power of our flawed humanity or it terrifies us and we stay down.

Loneliness is a self-imposed state
where we feel that we are not worthy
of others' attention. Or, they are not
worthy of ours.

"No" is the best deal of my lifetime.
"No expectations" means only surprises.
"No demands" means only gifts.
"No rules" means only choices.

You know those days when life and the world just sing? It feels great doesn't it? Guess what? That is how it is *supposed* to be!

Seeing our beauty and power as human beings can be terrifying. For once understood, we are called to square our shoulders and raise our heads as we claim this birthright for ourselves and embrace our responsibility to one another.

I had to live every moment of it—especially the awful parts—in order to believe life, know life, love life and make it my own.

Magic is worthless. Magic is smoke and mirrors. Magic is illusion and trickery. It's the miracles that knock my socks off and drive me to my knees in gratitude. And the miracles are there *all* the time. We just need to pay attention and be open to them.

"I'm gonna give it my all." Say what?

You were thinking of giving it your half, your three-quarter?

ON THIS DAY, let us stop thinking of ourselves as less. Let us simply know that we are more. More beautiful, more powerful, more amazing, more creative, more loving, more wonderful than we can possibly imagine. And this "moreness" is our birthright, our heritage and our future—on this day, in this moment and forever more.

If I strip my heart and my soul naked and stand before you, and you strip your heart and soul naked and stand before me, we will be looking into the eyes of our self-creation.

Honesty: Being full-bore, gut-grinding honest with myself, in my relationships and in my actions, is the bravest thing I have ever called myself to do.

Our ability to delude ourselves as to what is really going on in human relationships is amazing. Then there is that last piece—that one action or response—that causes all the pieces to fall into place. And bingo! Clarity arrives. We see the patterns, the actions and the truth. And it is time to let go and walk away.

It is more than interesting to me that once I make a final decision on something, quite often it is a very small thing that at last tips the scale. That final, seemingly little "Aha" is very clear, but the bigger events that came before somehow danced right past my radar. This is because, for some reason, I had been *choosing* to not see things clearly.

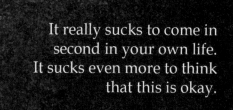

It really sucks to come in
second in your own life.
It sucks even more to think
that this is okay.

<u>A CHALLENGE:</u> Make a list of the people in your life who are important to you. How is each relationship going? Are you fully participating in it? Are there things that need to be said or actions that you should take? How do you feel about yourself in each relationship?

I now know that life is of me, through me, with me and in me, so all of my days are holy. And every thought, word, feeling and action are a call for me to bless this gift I have been given.

If we are lying to ourselves, is there any way for us to become aware of this other than the true gift of others telling us we are full of baloney?

And then, how do we come to the clarity and the courage to accept what they are saying as true? It takes a willing turn of heart, a push of soul and that grind in our gut as we admit, "Yes, you are right."

If someone in your life is blaming you for their misery, refuse to carry the burden. You simply are not that powerful.

Compassion is the working side of love. All love.

We do what we do. And we get what we get. If we don't like what we're getting, let's do something different.

Pity is an ugly sentiment. It allows us to weep great tears and wring our hands as we stand aside. Now compassion is a beauty queen. She demands full participation of our hearts and an "it's-time-to-get-dirty" use of our hands.

So much of what we call love is actually need. We need another human being to make us feel whole and valuable and good. It is our job to fill the need in ourselves by coming to love ourselves. Only then are we able to love another with an open heart, a giving soul and an accepting spirit.

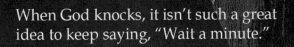

When God knocks, it isn't such a great
idea to keep saying, "Wait a minute."

ON THIS DAY, *may we see ourselves clearly. May we love the all that is us. May we share our gifts, shout our joy and embrace our faults. For it is in this "owning" of the parts of ourselves that we are not pleased with that we can choose to let them go. And so we become the creators of our own lives with conscious choice, honesty and compassion.*

Allowing others to abuse us causes two-sided damage. Our spirit is made smaller by permitting it, and the abuser is damaged by not being called on behavior that harms their spirit as well.

So when we stand up for ourselves, we also stand up for the person who is harming us.

The brutal despair and horrible loneliness of my used-to-be life is the greatest gift I have. For with unabashed honesty I can say to you, "Let me tell you my truth, so you can tell me your pain. Give it to me. I know it very well."

Then I can take your hand, hold your tears and walk with you. Your pain is mine. My pain is yours. We are no longer alone.

Receiving from others with grace, humility and gratitude takes practice. Then it becomes a gift we give ourselves and those around us.

Being an obliging sort of fellow, God is as big as we believe Him to be.

A CHALLENGE: Sit quietly and simply be with your self—that deep inside part. How do you feel about this person? Note the parts you like and the parts you don't. Accept all of them. And perhaps make note of just one that you would like to change today.

For more years than I care to remember, I went to bed every night with the vain hope that tomorrow would somehow be different. It was a vain hope because I never did anything different, you see. Then one day, even the hope was gone. And I faced the absolute truth that my life would simply continue as it was with me quietly dying inside each day as I pretended I was okay and that my life made sense.

It was this brutal truth that at last drove me to *do* something. I finally saw that I must choose a life that had meaning for me. I grabbed my God's hand, walked into change and have not looked back.

A closed mind and a closed soul seem to walk hand in hand.

ON THIS DAY, I wish you the courage to refuse to fold, staple or mutilate your heart and soul in order to please others. I wish you the clarity to not compromise your truth or your spirit in the hopes that others will love and like you. I wish you the wonder of throwing all that you have into doing this one day well—with kindness, grace, compassion, dignity, great love and hoots of hilarity.

The remarkable and horrible game called "Let's Pretend." You know how this game goes. Let's pretend I don't hurt. Let's pretend I'm not scared and confused. Let's pretend this is where I wanted to be.

I behaved and did the deal for years and years. But inside I was not happy. There was a quiet disappointment and a subtle anger. There was a gnawing, aching unhappiness. I wasn't supposed to feel this way.

I was sure that something must be wrong with me. My smile was stuck. My soul was stuck. My heart hurt. I should be grateful for my life. Others had it worse. I *should* be happy.

It was not until I finally had the nerve to admit my unhappiness, my anger, my confusion and my sense of despair that things got better. I stopped playing the horrible game of "Let's Pretend."

I got real, I got raw, I got honest, I got to work and I got me.

A matter of choice: I shall not bow my head and allow upset or self-caught depression to hold me. I shall not close down the light of my heart and stay in the dark. I shall not shutter my laughter or my joy in the shadow of a frown. I shall not dim the wonder of my own spirit as it is being called to celebrate the wonder of yours.

I'm really sorry, but you don't get "bonus" points in life for suffering or for martyrdom.

The pain of life is the creation point of its gifts. For from our sorrow come growth and change. Pain molds and carves us to wisdom and compassion as we walk through it with courage, grace and gratitude.

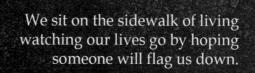

We sit on the sidewalk of living
watching our lives go by hoping
someone will flag us down.

I can live heart-sore or heart-soaring.

We were all dealt a hand in this life. The where we come from, the how we were raised, the blessing or curse of our family of origin. Each of us was taught the game of life by parents who were taught by their parents. If we don't like this game, it is incumbent upon *us* to change the order of play. It is up to *us* to create a new way to deal with life. This takes courage, honesty and the willingness to clearly see where we can do better than what we were taught.

To change our lives and our children's' lives, and the world itself, we must do better.

In hanging on to my pain, I am condemned by my own choice to revisit it again and again.

A CHALLENGE: What is the one thing that you are hanging on to that still hurts you? The something that someone did or said that you still remember and carry. What is the pinch and the rub, the moan and the ache that still bangs your heart and your head? Bring it forward one last time. Look at it. Know you cannot change it. Then consciously let it go. Repeat. Repeat. Repeat. Until gone.

My vulnerability, the sharing of my scarred heart and battered soul, is the greatest gift I can give you.

For in my quiet courage to share the real and often-broken truth of me, you may find your own. Then neither of us is alone nor are we afraid because there is strength in our shared frailties.

There is also laughter as we walk, and sometimes stumble, along together.

He who hesitates has another day to be miserable and blame others for the darkness and dullness of what he calls life.

It was when I at last answered this question, "Why me?" with the question of "Why *not* me?" that my life changed. That *I* changed.

Who was I to deny myself and those around me the beauty and wonder of my individual soul working and striving to know itself, to become more, to reach out with love and honesty to others?

Who was I to stay sniveling in self-pity and resentment? How dare I not take a leap and grab this gift and work to be a better person and share my heart with others?

What made me so special that I could hide the light of my life under a shroud of laziness and despair?

So I ask you, "Why *not* you?" This is your life. This is your gift to share and celebrate with others. How dare you not live it with all you've got?

To grow, I must continually let another level of self and ego go. And this can be excruciating. But as each subtle layer is at last laid down, the newly revealed inner core is finer, gentler and stronger. And this ever-growing ability to laugh, to let go of expectations, and feel all of life in me, through me, of me and with me, calls my soul ever larger and brighter.

Once we wake up, it is really, really hard to put the genie of awareness back in the bottle.

Our dreams are our hopes and aspirations. They are also what we are being called to give back through the talents and gifts we have been given.

Not so very long ago, if someone had told me how amazing and beautiful my life would become, I would have laughed in their face and then verbally kicked them in the teeth. God, that's horrible.

ON THIS DAY, let me bring all that I have to this day. Let me swing wide the doors of my heart and soul and say, "Bring it on!" Let me open my eyes and see the wonder around me—the people and the souls that walk this day with me. Let me smile from my heart and let my eyes crinkle with welcome. Let me listen with every ounce of my being to you and to the planet as it sings to me. Let me throw my spirit to this gift—to this life—with every ounce of me that I have. Because you know what? This is it. This is me calling all of me to the universe in delight and love.

To not tear the blinders off our souls, to not swing wide the gates of our hearts and explore the talents and the wonder of who we can be, is to spit in the eye of the power that created us. And worse yet, it is to spit in the eye of the person who is walking beside us.

For us not to try, for us not to take leaps of faith and follow our dreams and our intuition and our passions, is a slow death. For we are meant to be creative, we are meant to be challenged and to feel our hearts thump and our souls sing.

As creatures walking this planet, we are meant to stretch ourselves and toss our spirits out in question and wonder. If we do not? We shall know it. We shall feel the loss. We may not talk about it. We may even justify the not doing of it. But deep inside, we will know that we have made ourselves smaller by not having tried.

A CHALLENGE: Do one thing, just one thing, totally different today. Eat lunch by yourself or with others. Drive home a new way. Take a walk in a place you've never been. Smile at someone and introduce yourself just for the heck of it. Sing out loud!

I do believe it is our capacity to love
that perhaps scares us the most.

A negative mindset will always beat the hell out of you and your day. Guaranteed. You will also bore the hell out of everyone around you, unless you get other baloney-boys to cosign your attitude. Then, you get to all agree that life sucks and you are victims.

Happiness *is* the point. It is the only point. But we must understand fully that happiness is never a goal. It is a by-product of living with a full-wide, loving heart and gratitude driven soul. Then, it just seems to show up—sometimes in the most surprising places.

We wander around terrified that we aren't doing things right. What will people think of us? What happens if we make a mistake? So we bump into walls, fall down in a mess, blither and blather. And, guess what? The only person we really have to do it right for is ourselves.

When I am in pain because someone's behavior hurts me or makes me feel less-than, I must acknowledge that it is *my* expectation that is at fault. I expected them to behave differently. So let me accept the situation as an opportunity for growth. Because growth always follows pain, don't you see? When I can do this, the whole thing becomes a blessing. And gratitude shall mark me rather than tears.

Though, there are those times I *do* have to cry for a while. Yes.

Let us live with so much integrity and joy
that we are noticed most when
we are not there.

Sometimes we are encouraged to not shine—to not be as talented and powerful as we can be—because it makes other people uncomfortable. It makes other people nervous when we dance across life and roar with the delight of it all. To deny ourselves the wonder that is us, is a terrible loss—for ourselves and the world that needs us.

The true wonder of our humanity is not found in the grand gesture. It is found in the consistent day-to-day actions that quietly state our truth to the world.

ON THIS DAY, let's stop playing the remarkably, horrible game of "Let's Pretend." Let's get real. Let's look at one another and clearly see and accept each other. Let's talk about what is really going on with us. Let's share our hopes and our dreams. Let's look outside of our fear-caught isolation and truly see that the person beside us feels just like we do. Let's understand that we are so much more alike than we are different.

To see others clearly with compassion and acceptance is a tall order. But as I consciously look to understand you, I see myself. I see my soul working to do life well. I see my questions and pain, my sorrows and joys. So in striving to know you, I come to know myself as well.

My heart so hurts when I feel another's pain. My soul cries when I hear another's confusion and their agony in being lost. But I must refrain from telling others what to do. All I can ever do is have compassion as I look inside to where I can feel and understand what they are going through. And then I can make suggestions, always relating to what I did or what I have been through that is similar. And sometimes, to simply listen with all of me engaged is what I am being called upon to give.

Our children. They call to our hearts. They bring laughter and joy. They bring wonder and pain. And in them—and to them—our dreams are tossed out for testing and sometimes grief. But, they are ours. And there is always that place for their heads to rest under our chins. And for our smile to answer theirs. Here, gone. Now, tomorrow and forever.

My life is only limited by the belief that it can be.

To stand up for what I believe can be terrifying because I may have to stand alone. But to not stand up for what I believe is slow spiritual suicide.

It began with a single step—a decision backed by action. Then it was one foot in front of the other; then the next and the next. And now, I can turn my head and look back over the days and weeks. They have become years and the journey continues.

To not know ourselves is the deepest loss we will ever experience. And the saddest part—the difficult part—is that so many of us have no idea that we are actually missing in action in our own lives.

The power of one soul reaching out to another in honesty and compassion literally changes the world.

If I do not have the heart-soul courage and compassion to truly look at myself and accept myself, how can I ever hope to have any true intimacy with another human being?

You want to know the great thing about being totally comfortable with who you are? You can finally let your life rip and roar without feeling the need to explain yourself to anyone.

I must ride the wave of my life. I must widen my spirit and find balance in the power of the forces that drive my existence. For me, this balance comes from letting loose my desire to control the wave. Then as I spread my arms to let the wind of my heart and the sun of my soul breathe through me, there is joy and freedom—not angst and fear.

"I can't" so many times means "I choose not to."
Isn't it more honest and easy to simply state this fact?

Without follow-through, life is just a maybe, perhaps, sort of, kind of good idea.

We so often confuse need with love. Need grasps and demands. Love lets go and simply requests.

It takes great courage to tell others that we are hurt and in pain. It takes even greater courage to ask for help or comfort. But in being brave, our pain is lessened and we allow another person the gift of being able to give to us.

When I take myself too seriously,
life automatically stops being fun.
But I do provide untold
free amusement for others.

A CHALLENGE: Reach out to someone in your life today with total honesty. Tell them how you really feel—happy, sad, hurt, excited. And then, get really brave. Ask for a hug of comfort or celebration. You will be surprised by yourself and them.

If we don't have the courage to live our own lives, how can we make comments or judgments about how others are living theirs?

We each must find our own way. Each of us is called to live with honesty and courage as we find a road that fits our feet. Once done, our days of judging cease. We have no need to disparage or compare—for our lives are our own.

As our hearts get older, they become more capable of love, for they have been stretched, scarred and seasoned. They also learn a sometimes brutal wisdom that comes from having held so many others' hearts in the beat of their own. And it is from this wisdom the word, "No," must at times be spoken with enormous love and a keening sorrow.

The power of honestly looking into the eyes of another and revealing your soul without fear will change your life forever.

If I stoop to your level, I have settled for less. And my back hurts.

It is only through learning my own heart well that I can begin to understand yours.

There is such peace and power in accepting what life hands us. When I open my heart and simply say, "These are the facts. This is what I must deal with," life stops being a struggle and becomes a blessing of learning and wisdom, deep gratitude and simple joy.

If you really believe that life is too hard, then it is. And you have screwed yourself completely.

Often, the most powerful gifts I can give to another is my willing silence and my full presence in the moments of their life.

To ask for help takes great courage. To accept help takes willingness and humility.

I have been to the war zone of stupid-selfish living. I have survived and am proof that there is life after damned near dying there.

ON THIS DAY, I wish you an open hand to release your holding of the past. I wish you a gentle eye to see the wonder of this day. I wish you a grateful heart to embrace the joy of living. I wish you a wide soul to know fully the elegance and power of you walking this planet.

My sorrows and my disappointments can burn and tear. They wound my heart and cause my soul to whimper in dreams and unmet wants. But I am of the age at last to know that these shall pass. And in their passing these arrows of hurt leave wisdom, compassion and a knowing. My past and my survival become the strength and hope that I may someday be gifted to share with another.

Deep inside us all is a wanting ache for a meaningful connection to our own lives. We look for it in people and things, in careers and vacations, in entertainment and education. Funny thing? What we are searching for is already with us. It is us. All we need do is go on a fearless journey into ourselves and we will find what we are looking for. Guaranteed.

How dare we? How dare we think ourselves of no value? How dare we crawl into the shadows of life and complain that there is no light? How dare we not use our talents and our gifts? How dare we not share the wonder that is us with those whose lives we touch? How dare we spit in God's eye as we arrogantly damn ourselves with the easy label of "It isn't my job"?

To be authentic, to live my life with integrity, I must make sure that the person who walks in my shoes in public is the very same person who awakes with "bed head" in the morning.

What you see is what you get—all the time. And this person that I am keeps rocking and rolling with an open heart and soul as I grow and become more with every single breath.

What's worse than dying? Never having really lived. Major, major mistake.

I thought gaining wisdom would be a weighty affair. It isn't. The coin of its purchase is the pain of the past. And that burden has already been borne.

I just spent ten minutes trying to repair a disposable razor. Perhaps I should rethink my priorities? Laughing.

Like any habit, speaking our truth takes practice. Then, it becomes second nature. Then, it sets us free.

Our ability to experience joy is limited only by our conception of it. When we widen our idea of what happiness is to us, the world explodes in answer.

<u>A CHALLENGE</u>: Don't lie about anything today. Don't bend your truth. Be honest with yourself and others. White lies count. How does this feel? Notice anything about yourself?

When I am angry, judging or critical of others, I am actually damaging myself. For I must first create the energy of these emotions and then I must hold them in place before I can toss them at another.

"I'm fine," could be the two most self-damning words in the English language.

The more my heart and soul are torn and challenged, the deeper my understanding of and compassion for others becomes. Also, the more tender I become in my own strength.

ON THIS DAY, I wish you the courage to dance outside the circle. I wish you a heart that is joyful simply for the fun of it. I wish you laughter. I wish you a skip in your step and a bounce to your soul.

I find that now that the end of my life is within the realm of my understanding, I seek not so much to learn more about life as to know myself within my life. It is a "here and now" sort of thing rather than "someday later" sort of thing.

When I finally realized that the gut-weary fear that would sometimes crowd my sleep and haunt my dreams was really my own soul screaming at me, I decided it was time to wake the hell up.

Waking up takes courage, honesty and willingness. It is painful and brutal. But the pay-off is a life of clarity, joy, understanding, meaning and peace.

Something I have come to know and fully accept about myself—ordinary living bores the baloney out of me. I must live an extraordinary life. This means a life of mind adventures, of seeking, of discovery, of challenge. I must move and stretch and toss my heart and soul to life. For without this, I am a mere shadow of my own spirit.

I have to quiet my mind to hear my soul.

To believe that my life is a fling of fate—with no meaning or purpose—is simply no longer possible. The confluence of events, insights and heart-soul twangs that have bolstered me, driven me and consoled me into these years of my living, make that idea no longer even a dim meandering.

God's feet come walking unbidden and light. They always leave an impression.

It is our power that we fear, not our weakness. For our power as human beings—to create, to heal, to help, to love—demands that we stand strong and beautiful. And sometimes this also demands that we stand alone.

The joy and laughter of a child
aren't restricted to children.

To have the courage of my convictions is no longer a big deal. For these convictions have simply become who I am. Having torn my own heart asunder and ripped my own soul open, I at last know who I am. I am a child of this universe. I am meant to be here. All that I am is good and blessed. And my hand and spirit fly easily out in knee-bending gratitude and enormous love.

When I know not what to do, it is time for me to be still, to listen fully and trust that guidance will come.

The small gesture of our hand extended to another in love marks us as giants.

I have to put the bat to my shoulder and toss the ball in the air before follow-through is even part of the picture. Then I get to call the shot.

Our silence can be an angry scream. Our words of gentle truth can be a symphony of peace and understanding.

Please, please, never think of yourself as small or unworthy. For if you see yourself as this, how will others ever know? How will others ever see and understand and appreciate the gift that is you—this amazing and remarkable person that *you* are?

If life hurts, I know I'm not doing it right. I am trying to force things. I am trying to ram a round peg into a square hole. It is time to let go and allow life to happen. I am not in charge—and never have been. And that's a good thing.

If you are demanding, whiney and dissatisfied, please direct your energy elsewhere.

A CHALLENGE: Sit quietly with a piece of paper and a pen. Close your eyes and think about yourself—the inside you—for three minutes. Then write down at least three qualities you have that are the gifts you bring to the world.

There is no shame to be found in failure. But there is shame—and sorrow—in not having ever really tried.

It is in fully listening to others with quiet acceptance that I quite often hear the voice of my God.

Our capacity for "greatness" begins with the willingness and courage to think differently than the next guy.

When I truly look at you and you truly look at me, our souls are caught in that spot just between us.

What's the difference between an adventurous person and a sit-by-the-sidelines person? One says, "Oh wow!" and the other says, "Oh, no."

I can only be lost and alone in my life because I choose to be so. The path is always just before me. All I need to have is the willingness to set my foot upon it and the humility to ask for assistance.

In our desire for intimacy and trust we often refuse to see reality. We so need to believe in another's integrity, no matter what the evidence may actually show. So we allow the quiet damage to ourselves to continue as we willingly close our eyes—because seeing the truth is too painful.

ON THIS DAY, I wish you joy and a full heart. I wish you more questions than answers, more smiles than frowns. I wish you tears of gratitude and the laughter of a happy soul. I wish understanding and compassion for me and for you. I wish you this day to have and to hold, to live with every ounce of your being alive and in love with the gift that is you.

It is our demands and expectations that tie us to unhappiness. For we are looking for something to be *other* and totally missing the gift of what is. Life is the gift—just as it is.

If we don't like ourselves, we're screwed. If we don't love ourselves, we are screwed completely.

The most amazing journey of our lives is to fall in love completely—with ourselves.

If I become spiritually arrogant, I am of no use to anyone, particularly myself. For I have come to believe that I am more special than you are. Ouch.

We are lonely only because we have the misguided belief that it is possible to ever be truly alone. The power that beats our hearts and pushes our breath is always with us.

My fear-filled insistence on hanging on to people, places and things way past their expiration date screwed me for years. I am beginning to get a pretty good handle on the fine art of letting go.

You know that instruction manual
for life? Did you get one?

The stepping stones to success are what others would have called failures.

When I refuse to look at past pain—when I deny and run from the truth—I am condemned to live with a wound that never quite heals.

God needs us as much as we need Him.

Being "out of my mind" is the natural result of having fallen into my soul.

Don't you just love it when your smile and your heart and your spirit jump all at the same time?

When I view irritations as merely small inconveniences to ego, I can stay peaceful.

It is only through fully embracing the fact that I shall die, that I have come at last to really live.

To truly hate another human being, we must have a dead spot within ourselves.

Yes, you have an absolute right to choose to be miserable. And I have an absolute right to choose not to be around you.

"Let's Pretend" is a great game when we know it's a game. It's a mind-numbing, killing game when we don't have a clue we're even playing it.

Following our hearts and our souls takes great courage. But if we are to live awake and aware, this is what we must do.

My formal education is pretty much over. I am now on the lookout for those, who by their example, brighten my soul and waggle my curiosity. Then I tap them on the shoulder and ask, "Hey there, what the heck have you got going on? You want to share it with me?"

<u>A CHALLENGE</u>: Go up to that person you respect, admire or are curious about and ask them, "How'd you get to be the way you are?" They will happily share this information with you. If they don't, you are asking the wrong person.

If you are lost or in pain, I shall listen. If you are hurt and scared, my hand and heart will hold you. If your heart has been wounded, I will curl my soul into yours in comfort. But if you wish to hold to your sorrow, your pain or your hurt because misery has become your friend, I can only bless you in your decision as I walk on.

Being uncomfortable is a good thing. It causes me to sit up, take notice, ask questions, make choices and move into change.

If we are lying to ourselves about how we really feel about our lives, our lives will never be our own.

ON THIS DAY, I *wish you a smile that lights your eyes and causes those "crinkles" to glow. I wish you a heart that jolts in delight. I wish you mischief and laughter. I wish you the joy that comes from fully knowing that this is the best game ever invented—life.*

We are here for the joy of it. What other reason
could there possibly be?

Reaching for our dreams is our birthright
for they are the calling cards
of our tomorrows.

My life is stunning in the profound and simple truths that now hold my soul: love, willingness, honesty and compassion—for myself and for you.

We are the experts in our own lives. Once we come to truly know this and trust ourselves, life begins to make a lot more sense.

Have you ever noticed? We are often asked to believe in a "God" who is basically a screwed up version of a judgmental human being. And then we wonder why we don't like Him and are terrified of Him. Now that's funny.

I can't be the only one. The heaven I was handed as a youngster sounded really, really boring. And you know what? It still does.

What do we do when we toe the line and hit the mark, and we still aren't happy? Draw our own lines and make our own marks. You want to share my crayons?

Our intentions may damn us. But it is our lack of intention—our lack of awareness—that most assuredly damns us.

All of life is a game. You just might want to double check that you are playing the game you want to. Because, it really is your choice.

Guilt is a judgment and a burden that we hang upon our own heart and soul. Therefore, we are the only ones who can remove it.

How often do we say "no" to life before we have even thought of what would happen if we say, "yes"?

A CHALLENGE: Just for today make note of how many times you automatically go to the word "no" or another negative response before you even fully consider what you are being asked.

A spiritual life: What the heck is it?

It must start with an intimate and profound connection to my inner self, a quiet coming to that place where only *I* can go. This is the place where I must go to be fully happy and complete.

It is the place of *me* meeting *me* with clear eyes, compassion and acceptance. And from this vital place springs a wonder of understanding and depth that knows no bounds and never ends—a connection of *my* soul to the universe and to all of those around me.

It is often what we do not tell others that really matters. And it is what we do not tell ourselves that matters the most.

It is the lies we tell ourselves that do the worst damage.

When I fall in love with me, I am no longer desperately looking to fall in love with you.

You will never find it on the outside. It is on the inside. Every single time.

If we think life is a chore, it is.

Sometimes I doubt myself. Sometimes I question this path I have put my foot to. When this happens, I must check my motives. What is driving me? Is it ego or a true belief that what I am doing is about helping others? If my ego is in check, if it is taking second seat, then I am doing fine. The doubt is really fear of the unknown. I must place my hand and my trust in my God, reach out to others and simply keep putting one foot in front of the other.

Disappointment closes the door on what is as we bemoan and complain about what isn't.

When I learned to see the blessing in all things, my life changed completely. Now, even what others would deem as tragedy is a gift—of courage, growth, wisdom and understanding.

What would have happened to me if when my soul blinked awake there were no others there to welcome me? Being there for others is the gift and the blessing of awareness.

The biggest hurts
we do are so often to ourselves.

I thought my people-pleasing was about you loving me. It wasn't. It was about me needing to feel real. So, I made myself into the image of the person I thought you would find likable.

For me to truly see, I must open my vision. I must widen my frame of view. I must expand all of me as I walk this planet. Living is a heart thing—a grasping of my pulse-beat and wrapping it around all that touches me. Living is a soul-explosion thing. I must open my spirit and let life come into me—welcome it and hold it close.

Living is a reaching out and a touching back of everything around me—the world, my body, your heart, the breath of the universe and the single sigh of my human essence always reaching to learn itself more deeply.

How often do we not tell someone how much they have hurt us? So a relationship suffers and dies because we are cowardly, arrogant or simply lazy.

If we believe our souls are immortal, we are living in eternity right now.

I am of an age and an experience to at last understand and truly know that each pain of my heart and tear of my soul is a gift in the making. For from each have I learned compassion and understanding for myself and for those who walk beside me.

Being loved for simply who we are is the most profound gift and the deepest responsibility. For we are asked to be more fully who we can be with each passing day.

Listening fully—with a quiet heart and a non-judging soul—is one of the most precious gifts we can give.

The cool thing about getting older and having some wisdom on board, is that the time it takes to see the blessing in a disaster is getting really short.

If my life was a straight rocket ship ride up, where would the adventure be? It's the nose dives and the face plants on the floor that make it interesting. I get time to appreciate the journey as a bruise heals. I get time to be grateful for my God and my courage as I blow my nose, gather my heart and my feet once more beneath myself, and launch myself again full-tilt into life.

To be a generous person, I must truly value myself. For where is the generosity in sharing something I don't care very much about?

To laugh out loud, simply for the joy of it,
without forethought or concern,
is the epitome of full-soul living.

If I am judging you, I must place myself on the scale of "good and bad" and judge myself as well. How else can I be better or worse than you?

All of our life is a choice. Every moment we stand at decision about how we feel, what we think and how we are going to behave. When we know this, our lives become our own—to create or to destroy, to bless or to damn.

I am a child of the universe. And all the power of the stars and the planets rest at my feet and soar with my heart. In balance with the quiet roar of God's breath, my being sings and sighs with peace and a terrible joy.

A CHALLENGE: Think of someone you *really* don't like. Get a pen and make a list of at least three things about them that are actually good or worthwhile. How does your soul feel in working to be generous about theirs?

I cannot offend the God that breathes through my life. He is ever so much bigger than that. The only person I can truly offend or disappoint is myself. And this occurs when I get my outside confused with my inside. All of living must come from this inner source of loving energy that drives my soul.

All it takes for the adventure of life to begin is to say, "Yes!"

When I seek to always recognize the beauty and power of your soul, the beauty and power of my own soul rush out to greet you.

ON THIS DAY, know that you are powerful. Know that happiness is your birthright. Know that you are individual and beautiful in the person you simply are. Know that you are who you call yourself to be with each thought, each decision and each action. Know that no one can take any of this away from you—ever.

When I started shaving my legs simply for me, I knew I was on my way.

When we at last understand that we are each God realized, life gets really, really beautiful, really, really powerful and really, really fun.

The creative power of the universe sparks to light in our thoughts and minds. Where we dream is the place where our imaginations go to dance with our spring-shot hearts. So who are we to say, "I will not go there? I dare not go there?" For in our dreams are the realities of our future first glimpsed.

My God is like a balloon. He is as BIG as I breathe Him to be!

"Change" is a word that does its best work wearing a sweat suit.

The size of my heart is in direct proportion to the clarity of my soul.

Robin's rules for happiness:
1. Don't take myself seriously.
2. Don't take life seriously.
3. Don't forget #1 and #2.

There really is no secret to life. Each of us must find our own way. For me this means paying attention, actively seeking answers and striving for purpose and meaning in my days on this earth. This is often found by simply sharing myself—the good and the not so good parts of me—fully and honestly with others.

Have you ever wondered about how much energy it takes to be miserable?

Bounce back. What I put out to the world always bounces back to me. Life can only reflect back to me what *I* put into it. Ouch or awesome!

If you are not having the time of your life, whose time are you having?

If I am not gut-level honest with myself about my motives and emotions, then I am of no use to anyone at all, especially me.

The outer part of us is powered and driven by our inside part, yes? Then how come we choose to pretty much ignore this inside part?

Wisdom comes from taking the beatings life gives us with courage, humility, compassion and a sense of humor. It comes from a willingness to face ourselves and life head-on, never dodging the bullet or blaming others. And it also comes from simply getting up again with gratitude that we are able to.

Why on earth do we feel it is important to prove our point of view? It is ours. Isn't that enough?

There is really no such thing as failure when we give something all we've got. Things simply did not go as we expected.

The person who keeps us from having a remarkable life is us. Because we believe we can't or that we are not worth it.

In my experience, opportunity never comes knocking. She just sort of comes strolling by and says, "Ya wanna?"

I could only start "fixing" my life when I realized that I was the one who had broken it. I had done this through poor decisions, laziness, blaming others and not being willing to walk through the pain of growing up.

"But you don't understand!" This is the cry that we so often call to one another as we turn away—in despair, anger or disappointment—sure that no one else knows our hearts.

Let us not turn away from one another. Let us not allow this cry to go unanswered. Let us reach gently towards one another with open hearts and compassionate souls. For it is in truly listening to another that we at last begin to hear ourselves.

All skill is honed and crafted by mistakes. Mistakes are the learning tools of living. Let's honor them and welcome the gifts they bring.

When I am guided by a firm and honest connection to my soul, I always know what to do. My tread is sometimes wobbly as I step on new ground, but it gets firmer as my courage and confidence grow. And this growth only comes when I have the willingness and faith to keep on moving.

There is only *one* of us here.

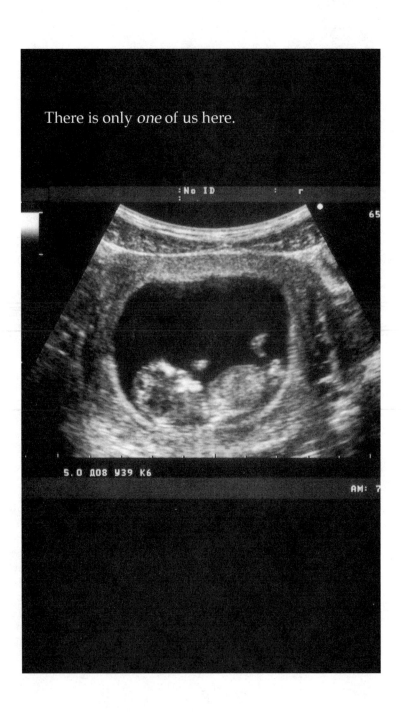

If I truly believe that someone else can make me feel miserable, I am in terrible trouble. I must realize that I am responsible for my own feelings, thoughts and behaviors. Then I call the shots, I direct my day and my God walks beside me laughing as we go.

When I am uncomfortable or unhappy, I am the problem. Always. It's not them. It's me. All ways.

What's one of the great things about being spiritually centered? You still get knocked off your feet at times, but recovery is only a matter of hours or days—not years or a lifetime.

ON THIS DAY, know that you are amazing, remarkable, cute, sexy, funny, smart, loving, kind, hilarious, generous, silly, goofy, wonderful, interesting, outrageous and totally, coolly God's gift to the universe! And you know what? So am I.

My God enjoys me just as much as I enjoy Him. I come to know myself through Him and Him through me. This makes for some really interesting and frequently hilarious conversations.

I encountered a huge stumbling block on my road to self-awareness. It was me. I was the one standing in the middle of the road, refusing to get honest and get to work.

A CHALLENGE: Sit down and get quiet. Sit down and get honest. What is the one thing that still makes you feel stupid or foolish? What is the memory that still makes you cringe? Open it up. Look at it. Accept it. Honor the truth of it. Forgive yourself. Laugh with yourself. Know you are human and let it go.

We are right here and right now. There is nowhere else to go and nowhere else to be but here—where our feet are.

Unnoticed and swift, selfishness and ego creep in. And the days of our own making become long evenings of quietly desperate unhappiness.

To speak our truth, we must first acknowledge it and own it in our hearts. Then, no one can cause us to wobble or second-guess ourselves, for we are centered in who we are.

It is all so very simple. It isn't easy. But it is simple.

For years I woke each morning in quiet dread, a bleared version of someone doing someone's life. It all just felt difficult and somehow wrong. I no longer feel this way.

Now each morning dawns as a jewel of gentle discovery—a wonder of delight at the newness that awaits me. There is also a love for myself and life that often truly brings me to tears.

Consciously or unconsciously we
must choose. And choose we
do—with our every thought,
feeling and action—every moment
of every day.

Peace—inner tranquility—is a very active choosing thing, not a sucking-my-thumb hoping and wishing sort of thing.

Often, my heart is blown wide in sorrow, in loss at another's self-brought anguish. But this pain scours my heart always to more compassion.

The cool thing about telling you my truth is that I only need to say it once, and I never have to raise my voice.

For years and years I spent my mind worrying the words, "If only..." If only, I had not married Bozo. If only, my children loved me more. If only, I had this thing or that thing.

Now my thoughts go to, "Only if." Only if, I make the choices and get my butt moving. Only if, I continually grow and change and reach and stretch my heart and soul. Only if, I show up in my own life each and every moment.

Then, my days are mine to create and my life is mine to sing. My heart can reach to yours, and we can do this this thing together.

I have come at last to a place in life where I fully know that these hours ahead are mine, as are all the moments of the rest of my journey upon this planet. I choose to embrace each breath with all of me involved. For in doing this, I am creating myself to be fuller and more beautiful.

Let my thoughts be direct and calm. How shall I be 100% in each moment? Where can I be of service? Where can I shine my joy? Where may I welcome a hurt heart or share a happy spirit? Let each moment of this day be one of gratitude, awareness, kindness and love—for me and for you.

We can only call as much life to us as we are willing to celebrate

I find it interesting and very comforting, that as I grow inward and become more aware of the immensity of my spirit, the outward aspects of living have become so much easier to walk through. The pinch and pulse of life that used to keep me always kind of dancing—and sometimes tottering—as I struggled to keep my balance, no longer have much power over me at all. There is a quietness to life that has nothing to do with the outside. It has everything to do with an inside me where silence walks with the profound echo of a heart coming home to itself.

For me to change and grow, I must be willing to continually check my ego at the door.

A CHALLENGE: Call yourself on your own B.S. today. Where are you being arrogant, a know-it-all or lazy? Where are you doing the reverse: hiding and calling yourself small and unworthy?

When we have the courage and willingness to do the work, to put aside our doubt and our fear, we become heroes and giants walking this planet.

If what I bring to others is my ego rather than my heart, I have abandoned them and locked myself within the lonely walls of my self-pride.

Before I can reach out and grab your hand, I must trust that it is there.

We are the star in our own lives. Who else possibly could be?

It is in the quiet of my soul that the universe comes calling. And the power of what it means to be totally human walks mightily in my being. For I have the power to create myself always as more beautiful and honest or to damn myself with self-deception and denial.

It is in my faults and failings that my strength is fully realized. For these I can acknowledge and choose to change. And as I discard these, I join my being with the same power that pushes a star and calls the tide to shore.

I know that I am a child of the universe, a part of all that is. So I am truly part of you. This gives my every action, thought and feeling profound importance, awe and meaning.

ON THIS DAY, Let us be bold and inside-brave. Let us share who we are with openness and joy. Let us know that we are each miracles walking upon this planet and that the person who walks beside us feels as we do. Our hearts are meant to be open, willing and free. Let us look to one another with acceptance and grace. Let us be compassionate and kind. For as we invite others to be as they are, we give ourselves full permission to do the same.

We aren't called to life so much as we call ourselves to live. We shake our souls awake. Then, we stand full tall, compassionate, open and brave— one next to another.

If I do not see myself in you, I am not paying attention or I am totally delusional.

When I think about my words before I say them, I walk behind the words to the thought. Then comes the question: Is this thought worthy of me? Of my soul? Of my heart? Perhaps silence is a better choice?

The entire thing, the whole shebang is completely driven by how *we* perceive ourselves within this thing called "Life." We truly create it all through our thoughts, feelings and actions.

The funniest part—the saddest part—is that we refuse to acknowledge this because it is often just too simple for us to wrap our minds around.

My life is no longer about what the "other" guy did. It can only be about what I did and what I choose to do. So simple and so much easier!

Who we are—our strength, our beauty, our wonder—will occur. It must because there is nowhere else to go and nothing else to do, but become.

I now understand that everything in my life—my breath, my body, this moment—are on loan to me without interest or payment due. So the choice and the responsibility of doing life reside in me. I can play "Screw it!" and not care. Or, I can run with it and celebrate the gift with everything I've got.

I must never impose my will on another human being, for even God refuses to do this.

A CHALLENGE: Take an honest look at what is pinching you and making you unhappy in your life at the moment. Are you possibly trying to control someone? Are you asking that someone do your will? And how is this working for you?

Inner peace is a spring board
for the mind and heart to soar
unfettered into places not yet
imagined or embraced.

Living in my head just
made me a wise ass.
Living with my heart and
soul wide open makes me happy
and sometimes really, really silly.

When we believe our pain to be special and unique, we damn ourselves to isolation and deny others the benefit of our wisdom.

We are so much more the same than we are different, especially in our experience of suffering. It is not the *what* that happened that is important. It is the *how* we feel about it that is.

The *what* is the drama of specifics. The *how* is humanity lived and survived.

The cool thing about living soul-wide and spirit-broad is that it is never too late to start. All we have to do is open our minds and jump in.

When I hear myself using the word "you" a lot in my conversation, I must take notice. Am I telling you what to do, think, say or feel? This is always a reality check for me. It also makes it kind of interesting when I stop talking mid-sentence to ponder the question.

It is only when I truly know myself to be beautiful, powerful and so very tender in my own humanity that I can embrace and honor these very same qualities in you.

A light heart and sparkling eyes are the signposts of an awakened soul.

The hour of our discontent is always of our own creation and our own choosing.

If I have to walk over you or take advantage of you to get where I want to go, where I want to go isn't worth getting to.

It is in silence that I hear the universe breathe. It is in stillness that my heart explodes in love. It is in calmness that my sight enfolds the world. In this peace, I find a powerful ally, an intimate friend and a joy-filled partner—me.

I'm really glad my God has an amazingly good sense of humor. He created me.

When I am judgmental, critical, angry, dissatisfied, resentful, arrogant or unhappy, the place where divine love belongs is crowded with some really deadly stuff. And my ability to love myself and others is pretty well shot.

God gives us free will to create
ourselves within our lives any way we
want. We screw it up and then we go
running to Him to save us and protect
us from the world we have created.
Kind of wacked, huh?

A knowing. I have grown roots into the ground and the sky. I am a mirror of it all. I have come completely home. My feet walk the trails of stars as my fingertips reach to touch the planets. My heart cradles the earth as the universe calls my name.

I wonder. If I had known that the myriad terrors and stupidities of my past would be the driving forces of this future I am embracing now, would they have hurt quite so much?

Probably not. I would have seen them as the blessings they actually were and have grown into myself a heck of a lot sooner.

<u>A CHALLENGE:</u> Take a quiet look at your own behavior with others. Are you complaining and negative? Are you light and loving? Do you bring a smile to others and to yourself?

It is only dissatisfaction with ourselves that drives us to dissatisfaction with life.

I can no longer co-sign your B.S. I refuse to be complicit in your self-delusion and self-destruction. It hurts me, and it's killing you.

To find true peace, we must go to war with ourselves and totally surrender as we willingly lay the weapons of denial and self-deception down.

The good thing about being a reformed "bad girl" is that I know how bad it can really get. And I have also learned to make good use of some of the stuff that made me really good at being bad. Things like audacity, passion, desire, imagination, determination, laughter, courage and getting up again and again, have come in really handy.

All real progress is born in the imagination, courage and pain of the women and men who refuse to settle for life as it is "supposed" to be—the renegades!

A lie, in order to stand, needs many like itself to support it. The truth needs nothing but itself.

How very interesting the human being is. He will look at you and tell you, "This is killing me." Then he picks up a shovel and digs in for another shovel-full of the very thing that is putting him in the grave.

Every soul in the universe intuitively knows it is divine. Our pain and "lostness" come from not believing we are worthy of this divinity.

Have you ever noticed how a truly happy person just kind of glows, that their joy and peace are like a magnet calling to your heart and your smile?

ON THIS DAY, I wish you a vision. I wish you to see the immensity of this gift we all have—this life. I wish you the punch and the joy of it. I wish you the laughter and the journey of it. I wish you the ache of your heart soaring in gratitude for the little things and the willingness to reach for the big things. I wish you the vision of peace and the knowing of love. I wish you to claim this person you are—amazing, remarkable, and so very beautiful.

Our belief that we are separate and apart; that our thoughts, feelings and actions are isolated instances of no import to anyone but ourselves is an illusion. This means that these characters on the page literally change the universe. They do. I have been changed by thinking them. You have been changed by reading them. And on and on it goes. How profound. How simple. How elegant. How powerful. We are!

ABOUT THE AUTHOR

Robin Korth, BA, MSN, is a renegade and an outlaw. She is also an international speaker, writer and businesswoman. Number four in a family of seven children, she grew up in the 1960s uncluttered scrub palm neighborhoods of Miami, Florida. In 2013, Korth launched her information and blogging website, which generated more than 12,000 followers on Facebook in its first six months. She also introduced the "Robin in Your Face" daily motivational app, which has been downloaded thousands of times across the globe. She is a divorced mother of two, has a friendly rescued dog named Scruffy and a self-assured cat named Sean. For more information, visit RobinKorth.com